A Trip to th[illegible]ty

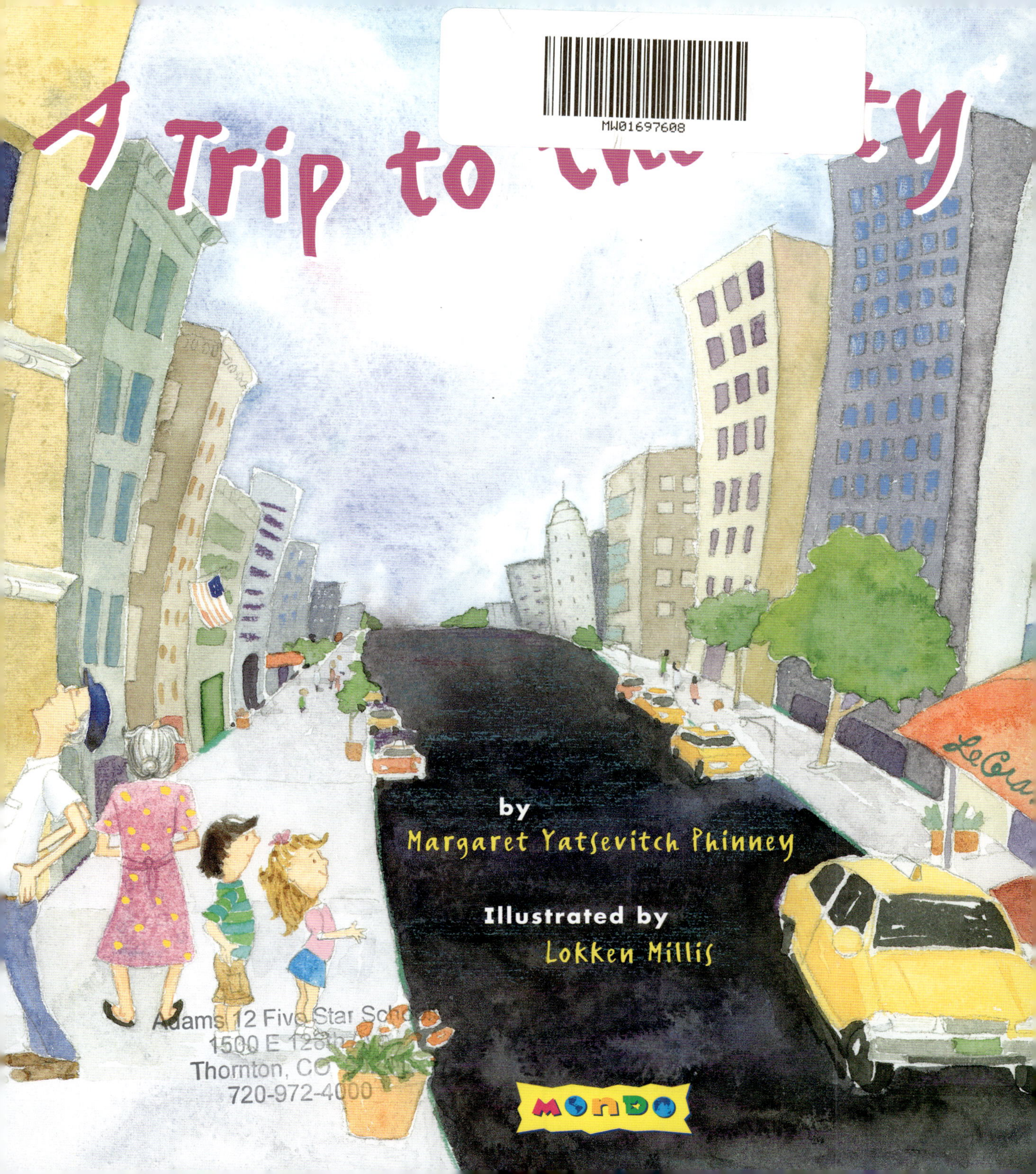

by
Margaret Yatsevitch Phinney

Illustrated by
Lokken Millis

MONDO

We are feeding ducks.

Grandpa is feeding ducks, too.

"No, Grandpa, no!" said Grandma.

We are looking at a big dinosaur.

So is Grandpa.

"No, Grandpa, no!" said Grandma.

We are waving for a taxi.

We see Grandpa waving, too.
"No, Grandpa, no!" said Grandma.

We are going up to the top.

Grandpa is going to the top, too.
"No, Grandpa, no!" said Grandma.

We are shopping at the toy store.

Here comes Grandpa.

"No, Grandpa, no!" said Grandma.

We are going under the bridge.

Grandpa is going under the bridge, too.
"No, Grandpa, no!" said Grandma.

We are putting mustard on a pretzel.

Grandpa is putting mustard on a pretzel.
"No, Grandpa, no!" said Grandma.

“We are going home!” said Grandma.
“Yes!” shouted Grandpa.
“We are going home.”